Grace-Filled Beginnings:
An Advent Devotional

John W. Stevens

DEDICATION

Pastors Paul, Tom and Barb -
three pastors that taught me about Grace.

Introduction

In the beginning, there was Grace.

It might have looked like the God of the Universe creating life and taking delight, and... it was Grace.

You will notice through this devotional, I capitalize the word, "Grace." Perhaps that seems conceited, and it might bother some people, like I am naming a fourth person of the Trinity. Perhaps that would be correct, and not to be argumentative, but I am not sorry about that.

Grace seems, for me, to take on a life of its own, and it becomes the energy that bonds the Trinity together. As the Creator, Sustainer and Liberator start to dance so fast, interweaving with one another, Grace is seen as waves of light, shining brightly and reaching out to grab hold of you. God's Grace washes over you.

In the manger, Grace was born, and became flesh. As Eugene Peterson translates the beginning of John's Gospel: "God moved into the neighborhood!" This was Grace-filled Beginnings.

God has been pouring out Grace from the very beginning. Again and again, we see this throughout scripture. The breath of God moving over the waters, as stated above. God's Grace also creates new beginnings in our lives, making us new again, filling us full of love, mercy and forgiveness.

So, come take a trip with me through some of the daily Revised Common Lectionary scripture passages assigned for the season of Advent. In our journey, I truly hope that you experience Grace anew, again and again. May God help you see the Grace in this season, and may these days be Grace-filled Beginnings.

Pastor John W. Stevens
Zion Lutheran
Oregon City Oregon

1st Sunday in Advent
Luke 21:25-36

"Be alert at all times..." - Luke 21:36a

"The hand is quicker than the eye." - Every Magician on Earth

I am a magician. A card shuffling, behind the ear coin pulling, rabbit out of a hat, magician. I have been a magician for longer than I have been a pastor, and truth be told, if I am on a flight with someone and they ask me what my profession is, and I don't know if I have the energy to explain my calling as a pastor, I will say that I'm a magician.

You probably have heard the phrase above, about the hand being quicker than the eye. I will let you in on a secret. It isn't true. The hand is not quicker than the eye. Rather, the magician makes you look at a different place when a certain move is taking place, making it seem like the hand is very very quick. We do it intentionally, but there are times when it can happen in quite the opposite manner.

When we read this part in the Gospel of Luke, we can be looking at one place, and looking so intently, that we forget to see the larger picture. We draw in and we read the passages that might elicit fear, all the while forgetting to step back and see the larger picture that God has been creating from the beginning.

Grace-filled beginning is how God works. When we get fooled, or feel like we missed something, it is helpful to explore the entire story of Grace, starting with the baby in the manger.

God isn't in the fooling business. From the very beginning, God is all about telling us this truth: Grace is found in the manger, and God is for us.

Prayer: God, remind us that You are not in the fooling business. Help us see that Grace is not a trick and is ours from the very beginning. Amen.

Monday
1 Thessalonians 3:9-13

Love wins.

Read the scripture again, and ask yourselves, "How could I think that love does not win?"

There are terrifying things in this world, and it is easy to forget this truth: Love wins.

Why does love win? Because love is from God. And God wins.

And here is a harder truth to hear: because of the Grace of God, we are enough. Or in other words, we win.

I find this to be fascinating and, for me, at least, true. I can read, "Love wins," and be all gushing with sentiment, but if I read, "We win...." things come to a screeching halt.

Because of the Grace of our God, we are called to love for one another. When our loving falls short, as is known to happen, God, shows us what love looks like again and again.

That is because Grace always wins. This has been the very truth from the beginning. God's love, seen in the manger, is the beginning of Grace. That Grace will continually claim, restore, and remind us once again that we are loved, and because of that truth, we love.

Thanks be to God.

Prayer:
God, help me remember that love wins, and because of that, I am enough. And help me when I struggle to believe that.

Tuesday
2 Peter 3:1-18

Earlier this year, I hiked Mary's Peak, which is outside of Corvallis, Oregon. There are amazing creation stories told by the Kalapuya people, tied to this mountain, and the fact there are signs of wildflowers, and memories of animals that are not usually seen in these parts shows the truth contained in the telling. The stories of the people whose land we hiked upon tell how this happened long ago, as one might say, "In the beginning..."

"You should remember words spoken in the past," the author of 2 Peter tells us. We are called to pay attention to the promises of God, and the steady work that God has been doing from the very beginning.

One might use the word, "slow," instead of, "steady," because it might seem as if God's actions can be slow as molasses sometimes. Hindsight gives us a different way of seeing this journey. Sometimes we can't see the length of the road we have traveled until we come to the end and look backwards.

It wasn't until I was at the top of the Mary's Peak that I could see how far we had come, and the beauty that was contained in the rolling hills, the wildflowers. The view of the rippling valleys and mountains that Mary's Peak afforded us was a reminder to stop and take a look at the past.

"Remember words spoken in the past," could be a mantra we use when it comes to the Advent Season, and as we remember Grace-filled beginnings. God is at work in our lives, though it might be difficult to see some days. However, if we stop, and take a look backwards, we will see that God has been guiding and walking with us from the beginning.

Prayer: Grace-filled God, help us see You walking with us. Help us recall the Word of the past, present and future, found waiting for us in the manger.

Wednesday
Revelation 22:12-16

My strength has always been in writing beginnings. I love beginnings where you can paint a picture and lay out the road map where we are going to travel. My endings are sometimes in need of work, however! Just ask anyone who has heard me preach. Years ago, one congregation member said, "I can't make my grocery list when you are preaching. I never know when you are going to end."

Whether they meant I never end, or my ending comes abruptly, I found myself laughing. In reality, there are the endings that only seem like endings, but in reality, they are the beginning of something new. These endings are in themselves Grace-filled beginnings.

The 22nd chapter is the last chapter in the Book of Revelation, and within these last verses of the last chapter of the last book in our scriptures, we also get a sense of Grace-filled beginnings, Grace-filled endings, and Grace-filled in-betweens.

Revelation is a book about worship, and our calling to worship the Lamb. Following the theme of worship, when we hear the Postlude, the final piece of music, we might assume that is the end. However, it is but the beginning.

We have been fed on bread and wine; body and blood. We have heard the Grace-filled Good News. And then we are sent from worship, into the world, so we can begin again, sharing the Grace of our God.

May the God of Grace-filled beginnings, remind you that God continues to make all things new - and that includes you!

Prayer: God of Grace-filled beginnings, renew my heart; renew my feet; renew my walk with You. Amen.

Thursday
Psalm 90

Thinking about yesterday, I am stuck on this idea of following the story through to the end. Reading the beginning lines, and then following the thread to where the last verse is punctuated.

Beginning with, "You have been our dwelling place in all generations," and ending with, "Let the favor of the Lord our God be upon us," like I'm wrapped in the Grace of God.

There are verses within this Psalm that give me pause, and as I wonder, I have to sit with them. Yet, I am reminded that Psalms are poetry, and just as life has its ups and downs, our journey with God has its ups and downs.

God is our dwelling place. What amazing words those are, and a sentence that could be a refrain to fall back on, or to return to, again and again. Grace-filled beginnings start with the understanding of God who wants us to be home in God's presence.

When life gets out of control, and it seems that God's hand is out to smite us (oh, isn't that a frightening phrase!!!), we can return to the beginning and remind ourselves that God is our safe place, our dwelling place. One place we find that safe place is the place where Martin Luther found comfort when he felt tempted or lost. He would clothe himself in his baptism daily, returning to the beginning, where God's Grace found him.

Grace-filled beginnings, ones which we see in the Manger, remind us that God not only creates a safe place for us, and is our dwelling place, but also becomes Grace in the flesh. God literally becomes the Grace-filled beginning in the babe swaddled and placed in a feed trough.

That feeding trough became a dwelling place for Grace!

Prayer: In the in-between times, it is easy to forget that You are our safe place, our dwelling place. Help us return to the beginning, where You find and claim us, in the waters of baptism. Amen.

Friday
Luke 1:68-79

I don't like being afraid. I am not a fan of horror movies, or stories that the narrative arc causes me discomfort. Give me a storyline I know really well, and that is just fine by me. Because of this, I can understand Zechariah's hesitation to be all in when the tradition he is familiar with gets changed.

The unknown can be scary.

When I become afraid, or unsure of what is going on, I find myself saying the most ridiculous things. A friend from years ago, when asked about things said to her concerning the death of her child, would just say with a shrug, "Death brings out the dumb." When we hear things that make us uncomfortable, whether that speaks to a new experience or perhaps old wounds, we can experience saying dumb things.

Because of that, I believe it is a gift when we are able to be silent, whether that is by choice, or in Zechariah's case, brought on by God. I know I would do better to learn to take a moment before speaking.

This week, when you experience a new beginning, or you experience the need to have a hard conversation, practice being silent first. Take a breath. Take a walk. Spend time in silent prayer. Breathe in, and breathe out.

Prayer: Gracious God, help me to live into the art of listening. Help me hear You speak to my noisy heart, in this noisy world. Amen.

Saturday
Luke 9:1-6

I remember when we began to get ready for the trip to our family cabin, located outside of Dillon, Montana. If one caught a glimpse of the boxes, bags, suitcases, coolers, more boxes, a few more bags —let's not forget that other bag that we almost forgot—they might think we were going to stay for year. In reality, we were only staying there for a single weekend.

It made sense. We wanted to be prepared, and having our stuff with us would not only make us feel prepared, but it would also help us feel safe. That really is the bottom line, isn't it?

We want to feel safe. Our stuff gives us the illusion that we are safe. But in the end, the safety promised by our stuff is but an illusion.

The disciples have been given power to cast out demons and to heal, and yet they still need to be told to leave their stuff behind. Go with God, and nothing else. Why?

Because God knows that when we rely solely on ourselves, we will fail. The notion of pulling ourselves up by our bootstraps is, as mentioned above, an illusion. We can't do this by ourselves.

We, like the Disciples, are called to rely on the kindness of strangers. The welcome of those who have a similar sense of mission as ours. The compassion of those who have been called by God to watch for the ones that bring the Good News. The kindness to welcome those who in the end aren't strangers at all, but kindred spirits in the Gospel.

Before we take a step out in mission, let us reexamine the Grace-filled Beginnings that we see in this text. God lets us know we have been gifted with the Spirit. God lets us know, from that very Grace-filled start, God goes with us.

Prayer: God, help us set aside the illusion that we can do all of this without You. Remind us that You send us, and where You send us, You also go. This is Good News! Amen.

Second Sunday of Advent
Luke 3:1-6

In our neighborhood, a building is being torn down. It has sat vacant for so long that I can't remember what was housed in it before. There is a lot of noise, and big trucks are moving huge boulders. Across the street, toddlers and preschoolers hang on the daycare fence trying to see all the wonderful activity that is taking place.

In the beginning of preparation, it is exciting to see what is coming. There can be a sign that the construction company erects, announcing, "Coming Soon!!" Sometimes excitement follows, as the name of the store is well known. Other times, there is confusion, for that which is promised is unknown to the neighborhood.

John the Baptist is in a metaphorical construction zone. John announces that something new is happening, and it is time to prepare the way. Move the boulders, fill in the potholes, and make smooth the path for the coming of the Lord.

John is preparing the way. It is a beginning, though it happens after the birth narrative, it is a beginning that is setting the scene for Grace in the Flesh, the one found in the Grace-filled beginning in the manger. John is preparing the way for the beginning of Jesus' public ministry.

This Sunday of Advent asks us to pay attention to how God is preparing our hearts for the coming of Love and Grace with skin on. What needs to be moved, smoothed out, even removed to prepare the way of God coming to us? Remember, it is God that is doing the preparing, and we get to be part of that.

Prayer: God, prepare me for the coming of Jesus into my world. Help me be a stepping stone and not a rocky barrier for others longing to meet Jesus. Amen.

Monday
Romans 8:22-25

I have an addiction. This is different than my standard addiction to caffeine or the one that has me living one day at a time. No, this one is more insidious because it hides in the background, and unless you know me well, you would never suspect it.

I am addicted to stirring. That act of taking a spoon (in my case, a wooden spoon) and literally stirring the pot. Whether it is while making soup, pasta, candy, and even boiling a pot of water, I will stir it until you can't really tell what it is anymore.

I want the finished product now, and somehow, I think stirring helps me get to the finish line more quickly. No "watched pot" advice will deter my obsession.

What it boils down to (pun intended), it really is that I do not have patience, and the idea of waiting for the end product of the creation is really difficult. I need to see the fruits of my labor, and I need to see them this instant!

And truth be told, whether I can see it or not, God is doing amazing work. Grace-filled beginnings are happening all the time. Even before we see that which is a new creation, we are told that Grace is at work in, with, and through us. The very hope that God is at work is a sign of these Grace-filled beginnings.

Today, put down your metaphorical spoon, and pause. Take a moment to list the hope in your life that you have missed due to all the busyness of stirring. Take a breath and give thanks for those moments in your life that help lay out the story God is creating - your story - with the Creator of Grace present from the beginning.

Prayer: Give me eyes to see the hope that You have created and are creating in my life. Help me trust You.

Tuesday
Psalm 126

"Just you wait!"

Isn't that a scary statement? Have you heard this in your own life? "Just you wait... until..." Oh wow, my anxiety has gone through the roof just writing those words!

Those words, however, don't have to be filled with dread and worry. What if we read those words with a tone that echoed the tone of the Psalmist who penned Psalm 126??

Advent is a time of waiting, and of hope. Like yesterday, we are reminded that as we hope, God is still at work in our lives. The very presence of hope is an act and a gift of God.

The psalm for today, which gets named, "A Harvest of Joy," is packed full of hope, and is a reminder of Grace-filled beginnings; that God is at work in our lives, and has been at work before we even recognized it.

Read this psalm again and say the words, "Just you wait," once again. But this time read them in the tone of a caring parent, or the one that meets us at the beginning, with Grace. That Grace-Filled Beginning, known as the Creator, the Redeemer and the Comforter, finds us again in the middle, and at the end.

Through it all, God is moving and changing us, in and through Grace. "Just you wait!!" Indeed!

Prayer: God, help us wait with assurance of love, and the promise of Your amazing gift of Grace. Help us remember that You have been here from the very beginning, and continue to walk with us, giving us the gift of hope. Amen.

Wednesday
Luke 7:18-30

"Are you the one who is to come, or are we still waiting?"

One sits and waits.

The door opens and a person enters.

That person approaches and sits down with their cup of coffee.

And... that person is nothing like the person that was expected.

Nothing like expecting someone and finding out that from the beginning that they are WAY different than their online profile.

Jesus shows up, and his online profile, with job title, The Messiah, was nothing like John expected. John sends two of his disciples to ask the question: "Is it You?"

When God messes with our expectations it can be jarring, and it takes us a moment to get our bearings. God often acts differently than we might expect.

Yet, God has been acting differently than many think God should from the very beginning. Grace poured out, finding you where you are hurting and reminding you that you are loved is what God's online profile is all about.

Like a Wikipedia page that can be edited, throughout time, God's profile has been rewritten to give us a scarier version. For some, God will smite you if you don't act just right, know all the correct dances, or just happen to say the wrong thing. Because of this, when we experience Grace, it can be jarring.

Jesus is reminding us that Grace-filled beginnings are the norm, and it is what we can expect from the manger, filled with the One promised to be Grace in the flesh. And being jarred isn't always a bad thing, thankfully.

Prayer: Jesus, give us eyes to see You as you really are, Grace for the world. Give us hearts to see You as you really are, Grace for each one of us. Give us feet to bring that news to the entire world. Amen.

Thursday
Isaiah 12:2-6

"I will trust and not be afraid." - Isaiah
"I am shook." - Me

Isaiah lifts up these words, and they resonate with my heart. Not as something that I live everyday, but as a hope and a desire for the everyday. I want to be trusting and not be afraid. So I read this verse, which reminds me of the Psalm from yesterday, and these words rise to the top, calling out for me to notice.

When you have oil and water, and you shake them together, you can see them mix. I find that my life, which is a mix of fear and faith, certainty and doubt, works in a similar way.

That phrase, "I am shook," reminds me of when aspects of my life are mixed up, like oil and water and intertwine. It gets hard to separate one part from another. If I attempt to remove one from the other, the oil from the water, as soon as I am done shaking, it is impossible.

So, I stop. And I wait. I wait, and I wait.

You know what? The oil and water start to separate, and it seems as if it almost takes the form of what it was in the beginning.

Grace-filled beginnings sometimes are hard to grasp, because the world moves, things happen and we are shook. It gets hard to notice that which is in front of us the entire time - God's love and God's Grace.

We are called to wait and to pause. In that pause, we can start to see what rises to the top, and that is the promise God has made from the beginning: We are loved and wrapped in God's Grace. From the very beginning.

Prayer: God, help me pause, so my mixed-up soul may recognize You, since You been with me from the very beginning. God, help me trust You and not be afraid. Amen.

Friday
2 Corinthians 9:1-15

There is an ancient story about two travelers, walking at different speeds, who meet a farmer on the road.

The first one to come upon the farmer says: "I am traveling to the town that is just up ahead. What kind of people live there?"

The farmer says, "What kind of people were in the town you just left?"

"Oh, terrible, terrible, terrible."

"You will find the same kind of people there."

As the first leaves discouraged, the second meets the farmer on the road, and there is a similar exchange.

"What kind of people were in the town you just left?"

"Amazing and kind people. Just the best!!"

"You will find the same kind of people there," the Farmer replies.

God pours out God's Grace from the beginning and continues to pour Grace out. That is what God does. And for that I continue to give God thanks.
It is not dependent on you or me. God is God, and God's Grace is given by God. Thanks be to God.

Paying attention to the Grace and blessing God has put into our lives; and using those blessings for helping our neighbor and putting those blessings back into the world gives us eyes to see the Grace of God, that has been there from the very beginning, in the people around us.

God's Grace can help us write the next chapter in our journey when we stop and pay attention to the Grace given to us. Some might say, "Count your blessings," and to that I would say, "As well as the Grace which has laid the foundation of the world from the beginning."

Prayer: God, help me see in my neighbor the Grace you have poured out into the world. Give me Your Spirit, the Advocate, who not only helps me see, but changes the way I see the world around me. Amen.

Saturday
Luke 1:57-66

"Fear came over all their neighbors," ~ Luke
"I wonder..." ~ John Stevens

When God pulls up God's sleeves and start to act, or at least when we get to see very very very clearly that God is acting, it can be quite scary.

Early on in this devotional, we explored how Zechariah was forced to be silent and listen. In today's scripture reading, we see the opposite. Zechariah's lips are opened, and he praises God and tells the story from the beginning.

In this act, the unsealing of Zechariah's lips, the response from the neighbors is awe. They are afraid, and full of questions. The most prevalent one is about vocation. Luke writes, "All who heard them pondered them and said, "What then will this child become?""

Holy wonder leads to pondering for Luke. We will read (spoiler alert) about Mary's pondering when she visited by shepherds and the magi.

Pondering could possibly be the dance between Wonder and Grace. The movement between God's Grace-filled beginnings, and when we are swept up into the dance of salvation, with God taking the lead. Pondering can happen when we are questioning what direction or path God is guiding us. Wonder and awe are mixed with Grace-filled beginnings.

I invite you to spend time today pondering how God is at work in your own life. Read this scripture out loud to yourself, and listen for the questions and wonderings that lead to pondering God's Grace, who, in Christ, claimed you in the waters of baptism and finds you at the Eucharist.

Prayer: God, please quiet my anxious heart as You invite me into the act of pondering. Guide me to the questions that want to dance with my faith. Help me see the Grace You have wrapped me in, so my fears and awe lead to wonder and joy, expanding the holy art of pondering.

Third Sunday of Advent
Luke 3:7-18

"What then shall we do?" ~ John, the Baptist
"I have to do what now?" ~ John, the one called Stevens

I need to give up sugar. I need to exercise more. Uh... I need to start exercising. I need to pray more. Uh... I need to start praying. I need to read my Bible. Anxiety leads to fear which leads to flight.

John the Baptist has come on the scene and is calling people to holy living. The words, "You Brood of Vipers," call out to be made into a Hallmark Greeting card. In this third Sunday of Advent, as we wait, we again see John the Baptist pointing the way to holy living.

What does holy living look like for John? Does it look like the frantic phrases I wrote above? How do we start living "right" and following the "straight and narrow"? It might not be how we think, or at least all of it. I am not saying that those statements above don't have merit, but for John, they are not what riding the waves of baptismal waters is all about.

The question is asked, "What then shall we do?" (How quickly I can forget about the simple art of asking questions when I am anxious.)

Where do Grace-filled beginnings lead us? What does holy living look like?

For John, the Baptist, it involves the community around us. We are called to give of ourselves, for the benefit of community. Grace, from the beginning, is about the community being pulled together through love and inclusion. We see our neighbors; we notice their needs; and out of the calling and love that God has for us and the world, we respond. That is what we are to do.

Prayer: God, help me see my neighbors as lovable. God, help me see myself as lovable. Give my faith feet traction so I while I ride the baptismal waves of Grace, you carry me all the way to help my neighbor.

Monday
Philippians 4:4-7

"Peace of God, that surpasses all understanding, will guard your hearts and minds."

I have a shirt that says, "Science... like magic but real."

I love that shirt, because I love answers. I am not a fan of, "Because I said so." I want to know **why** we are doing something, even as much as **how** we are doing something. I am a fan of knowing how things work.

God's Grace, which was rolled out at the very beginning, leaves a lot questions. The author of Philippians reminds us that faith doesn't belong in a box labeled, "The Things I Know," and rather in the box, "Things I Wonder About!"

I love this scripture passage **so much**.

I love it all. I love the reminder to rejoice. I love that the author seems to know me so well that they tell me twice. I love the mental picture of gentleness outflowing onto conversations and interactions with others, and how that has a positive and holy influence on the world.

I love that we are gently reminded to lift up our needs to God, and resting in the peace of God, put anxiety on the shelf. And then to bring this all home, I love that we are reminded that all of this happens because of the Grace and Peace of God.

Not only does the Peace of God surpass all understanding, but even when we don't understand, our hearts and minds are guarded. I don't need to know how this happens. I don't need to be perfect for this to happen. You don't need the answers for God to show up and love you. God's Grace has been there from the very beginning, showing up WAY before we even knew about God or God's Grace.

Prayer: God, thank You for Your Grace, and for the peace You promise. Thank You that I don't have to understand **how** You work in order **for** You to work. Amen.

Tuesday
Hebrews 10:10-18

"I will remember their sins and their lawless deeds no more." - Hebrews 10:17

"Remember that dumb thing you did back in 3rd grade?" - Me, 12 a.m.

I have squirrels and they have cages. My squirrels set up shop and instead of just running around in my brain, making it hard to focus, they have set up a small little printing press to make newsletters full of news of the past.

"Remember when you did this??"

My midnight mind is set on remembering the detailed past of all of my mess ups. The times I made a complete fool of myself, which happens often. Especially if the event, when it happened, wasn't all that bad... through the filter of the midnight mind, it becomes an astronomical failure.

"I will remember their sins and lawless deeds no more," we read in Hebrews, and these are words that I should have embroidered on a pillow, so maybe I can take them to heart. Perhaps I can come to believe them through osmosis and helping my squirrels sleep.

Here is Grace-filled news: God doesn't remember. God intentionally forgets. God isn't like us and doesn't think of a Grey Elephant in Denmark when those words are mentioned. (You are thinking of a Grey Elephant in Denmark, aren't you?). God casts away our sins and remembers them no more.

Perhaps in the recognizing of that promise, we can start to live into letting some of our past horrific acts, like spilling milk in the middle of a cafeteria, go! (especially if they are made that way by our midnight mind). God has been in the forgiving business since before we were created. That is Grace-Filled Good News.

Prayer: God, help me forget the sins of my past. Help me believe that You have already forgiven and forgotten. Amen.

Wednesday
Isaiah 11:1-9

"A shoot shall come out from the stump of Jesse, and a branch shall grow out of his roots." - Isaiah 11:1

On the way to our cabin, outside of Dillon, Montana, there is a ridiculous but amazing sight. It is ridiculous because if you would have asked me the perfect to place a seed, this would have been the last place I would have picked. I use the word, "place," on purpose, because it really can't be planted.

It is amazing because, out of a large boulder, a very large pine tree has found agency and has grown, considering its size, for many years.

I read the good news laid out in Isaiah 11, and I know one thing for sure: I am glad that God doesn't ask me where to plant the seeds of faith, and the hope that is given through Grace-filled beginnings.

In today's reading, God reminds us that Grace-filled beginnings can happen anywhere, and at any time. In most stories, a stump signals the end of something. The tree has been cut down. The end.

And usually, that end is final. But not here, and not with God.

Like the seed that should have seen its last days, yet grew through and in spite of hard terrain, lack of good soil, and in the end, a lack of hope, God, through Grace, shows up again and again, and a shoot appears. In other words, New Life, and Grace-filled beginnings happen again.

We are getting closer to the time that Grace-filled beginnings are found in another strange place: A manger. God decided where this all would take place, and did not ask my opinion. For that I give thanks!

Prayer: God, remind me that You have given me new life and the twig of hope, and the seeds of Grace, continue to find root, and grow in us for the sake of the world. Amen.

Thursday
Jeremiah 31:31-34

Another way of stating, "Grace-filled Beginnings," to say, "The day is surely coming." There is so much packed into that phrase, "The day is surely coming, when…" We read it and we need to know what comes next.

"'The day is surely coming, when I will make a new covenant,' says the Lord." (Jeremiah 31:31a).

I love this verse *so much* because of one word "surely." (Don't call me, "Shirley!" - Thank you, Leslie Nielsen).

"Surely," in this context has certainty behind it.

God is acting, and God will act! This new covenant will be made, and God's promise is secure.

As I see it, "Grace-filled beginnings" work this way as well. God is acting, and God will act, and we get to be a part of it. From the moment the Holy Spirit moved over the waters and she breathed life into mud, all the way to when an incredibly tiny baby was wrapped in bands of cloth, God is covenanting with us in good and holy ways! God is always making us new and continues to make us new because of who God is, and who we are to God. We are loved, made new, and are enough because of God's Grace.

Prayer: God, thank You for Grace. Thank You for new beginnings. Thank You.

Friday
Psalm 80:1-7

A lament. A cry for help. A prayer that God might change God's mind.

Christmas Eve is coming. "Grace-filled beginnings" is showing in his mommy's belly. The donkey's back is uncomfortable, and they have been riding along feeling it all. And it makes me wonder.

I wonder if, from the time Mary sang her song of dissent against the powerful, and her words of God lifting up the lowly, she also lifted up prayers of lament, or cries for help.

The road to Bethlehem couldn't have been smooth, and the donkey didn't have the latest suspension, making it a cushy ride. Nine months pregnant, traveling to a place that Joseph and she had been ordered to go. I can only imagine that some choice... prayers... were offered up.

Mary, the mother of God, who carries "Grace-filled beginnings" in her womb, had to be tired, worn out, and, I would venture to guess, done. I hear this psalm and I wonder if Mary or Joseph might pray line after line to each other as they trudged along. "Restore us O God; let your face shine…"

This psalm is full of deep, raw, human emotion. This psalm connects Mary to the sojourners of the past, and it connects us to the pilgrimage of Joseph and Mary, the two entrusted with the care of God, Grace-filled Beginnings. This psalm, through those who pray it, connects us to God.

Prayer: The Psalm is a great invitation for us to write our own prayer of lament and hope as well as words of thanks for Grace who has, is and will always be present even before we start.

Saturday
Luke 13:31-35

I was given a Christmas gift over 20 years ago that seemed quite strange at the time. I unwrapped this long box that was shaped in such a way that a bow tie might fit inside. What I found when I opened it was a long nail that was rustic, long and old. It was a metal spike, with a note attached.

I don't remember the note, but I remember the overall message. This spike was a Christmas ornament that I was to hang deep inside the tree, where it couldn't be seen easily. It wasn't to be on display but it was to hang hidden, as a reminder to me that Christmas is ultimately tied to Easter.

This spike was to remind me that, in this story, the tree would become a cross. In other words, Grace-filled beginnings happen again and again. They happen in the manger, on the Cross, and in the vacated tomb.

The donkey that Jesus is riding, in the womb of his mother, Mary, on the way to the manger echoes another donkey that Jesus rides into Jerusalem.

"Blessed is the one who comes in the name of the Lord!"

Words that we will say on Palm Sunday, as Jesus enters the city, with his face set towards the Cross.

Actions that give us pause, break our hearts, and yet, in the midst of it all contain hope and Grace. Our God is a God of new beginnings, Grace being poured out and making all things new - again and again.

Prayer: God, as I remember how the whole story of Jesus is tied together, I give You thanks for Grace-filled beginnings. I give You thanks for all the ways You make my life new. Again and again.

Fourth Sunday of Advent
Luke 1:39-45

I have a friend from college who had so much joy, you couldn't help but feel joyful around her. She had a way of lighting up the room by just a single smile or a quirky statement that was so, well, joyous. Bad moods didn't stand a chance around her. Not because she was uncomfortable with your feelings, or purposely tried to change them. Her joy would find its way into your heart, and slowly soften it. Bad moods would convert into a joyous heart.

Joy is infectious, as we see it clearly in the scripture for today. Mary seeks out Elizabeth. We don't know how Mary was feeling, though we could probably guess. What we do know is she seeks the company of family; of those close; of those who might understand the news that has been brought to her. She seeks out Elizabeth.

As soon as Mary enters the room, Elizabeth knows. Or rather, the baby in Elizabeth's womb knows. And the joy of baby John in the womb overflows into a jump and Elizabeth is infected by this joy, and it overflows and is expressed with words of praise.

May our joy of the expected news of the coming Christ bring us similar joy as it did for Elizabeth, and her unborn child, John, who will grow into the man we know as John, the Baptist. May the news of Grace-filled beginnings, found in two unlikely mothers, then in two cousins, one the Message, and the other the Messenger, bring joy to your hearts and minds.

Prayer: God, thank you for the gift of Joy. May Your Joy find its way into our hearts. Help us share that Joy in word and in action this and each day, as we anticipate the coming celebration of Grace found in the manger.

Monday
Luke 1:46b-55

We are so close to the manger. If we were in the backyard, we might peer over the fence and see Mary and Joseph. But right before we get to the birth narrative, in the background, we hear Mary singing a song that fills us with holy courage.

Grace-filled Beginnings don't always sound smooth and calm. Mary's song is one of the most amazing pieces of scripture and found within it is the song of the resistance. We see a picture of a promised future being brought to fruition in and through the birth of Grace found in the flesh. We hear of a far-off future that is ready to be born in the present. In the manger, and in our present time, God is creating Grace-filled beginnings.

In the same song, in the same words, we find that while they fill us with hope and promise, they will strike terror in the hearts of the empire, the emperor, and those who sit in seats of power. These words remind us that God always stands on the side of the outcast, the poor, and the downtrodden.

We see the unwed mother, so very young, say, "Yes," to God who has asked her to be God's mother. How very powerful and yet scary this had to be for Mary. Yet, here she is, singing this song that we call The Magnificat, which we sing to welcome Jesus, the Grace-filled beginning, into our hearts.

Prayer: God, help us say, "Yes," to You when we are asked to bring Christ into this world. Help us speak truth to power, and to live the life the Prince of Peace calls us to with love. Amen.

Christmas Eve
Luke 2:1-20

My heart longs for You.
    Fill it with Your Grace, O' God.
Help me begin
    taking step by tentative step,
        fighting the fear that I'm not enough.
Help me begin
        walking on the ground You
            have been preparing
                from the beginning.
Fill me with Your Grace
  prepare me to be a messenger
        anticipating the day
          when I see You -
             wrapped in swaddling clothes,
             asking for a dollar,
             needing shelter for the night,
             walking into a church basement.
                Grace-filled Beginnings.

"The time came for Mary to deliver the child..."

      Help me
         walk in Grace and
            because of You,
            I begin again.

Made in the USA
Monee, IL
15 October 2024

68075211R00036